Conversations When
Death Is Near

~9C~

at the
edge *of* life

RICHARD L. MORGAN

UPPER
ROOM BOOKS®
NASHVILLE

At the Edge of Life: Conversations When Death Is Near
Copyright © 2014 by Richard L. Morgan
All rights reserved.

Upper Room Books website: books.upperroom.org

UPPER ROOM®, UPPER ROOM BOOKS®, and design logos are trademarks owned by The Upper Room®, a ministry of GBOD®, Nashville, Tennessee. All rights reserved.

At the time of publication all websites referenced in this book were valid. However, due to the fluid nature of the internet some addresses may have changed, or the content may no longer be relevant.

All scripture quotations, unless otherwise indicated, are from the New Revised Standard Version Bible, copyright © 1989 National Council of the Churches of Christ in the United States of America. Used by permission. All rights reserved.

Scripture designated NLT is taken from the Holy Bible, New Living Translation, copyright © 1996. Used by permission of Tyndale House Publishers, Inc., Carol Stream, Illinois 60188. All rights reserved.

Scripture designated KJV is from the King James Version of the Bible.

Note: All the names and conversations in this book have been changed to preserve confidentiality. These true stories record real conversations between family members and caregivers and actual persons as they are dying.

Cover image: © Balazs Kovacs Images/Shutterstock.com
Cover design: Left Coast Design, Portland, OR / www.lcoast.com

Library of Congress Cataloging-in-Publication Data

Morgan, Richard Lyon, 1929–
  At the edge of life : conversations when death is near / Richard L. Morgan.
    pages cm
  ISBN 978-0-8358-1332-7 (print)—ISBN 978-0-8358-1333-4 (mobi)—
  ISBN 978-0-8358-1334-1 (epub)
1. Death—Religious aspects—Christianity—Meditations. 2. Aging—Religious aspects—Christianity—Meditations. I. Title.
  BT825.M65 2014
  248.8'6—dc23

                                                                          2013049098

Printed in the United States of America

Contents

Dying Moments

Preface

Some time ago I was on my way to visit a church member who was near death at an inpatient hospice. I knew she had limited time. Her son, distraught and in tears, met me at the door of her room. His mother had just died. He looked at me with sad eyes and said, "Death ought to be the subject of your next book."

That was over twenty-five years ago, and my writing of other books has taken precedence. Since that time I have been present with family members and friends as they lay dying. I have experienced a sense of hopelessness, feeling overwhelmed as to what to say. However, through many years of experience and training as a hospice chaplain and volunteer, I have learned how either to be still or to carry on a conversation with those who are dying. These final conversations form the heart and soul of this book. It is for caregivers learning to listen to dying persons and talk with them. It offers help for those companioning loved ones on their final journey. I wrote this book in order to

- Help the living and the dying talk to each other.
- Be a valuable resource for family and caregivers to learn how to initiate and maintain conversations with the dying.
- Provide a guide for clergy and caregivers on how to listen to those who are dying.
- Use as a guide for congregations on how to relate to dying members.
- Become a way to face the reality of one's own dying and to plan for it.

I hope you will find that these final conversations remain a gift from those who are dying.

—Richard L. Morgan

ACCEPTING YOUR DYING

The Lord GOD has given me the tongue of a teacher, that I may know how to sustain the weary with a word. Morning by morning he wakens—wakens my ear to listen as those who are taught.

—ISAIAH 50:4

1 LISTENING TO THE DYING

Morning by morning [God] wakens—wakens my ear to listen as those who are taught.

—Isaiah 50:4

Millie, a nurse, knew she was dying from ovarian cancer. Her condition was hopeless. Yet, for the sake of Jim, her husband, she maintained a conspiracy of silence about her condition and played the "let's pretend game." For Jim's sake, she consented to painful chemotherapy treatments, bearing the pain, even when she knew the treatments were an exercise in futility. Jim, a loving husband, made every provision for Millie's comfort, even hiring an all-day caregiver.

As Millie's pastor, I made frequent visits to the hospital and to her bedside. I felt helpless to say the "right" word and dreaded the silence that pervaded her room. Her dying made me uncomfortably aware of my own death, for which I felt unprepared.

As I prayed for guidance, the Spirit led me to the words above that describe the work of the Servant, and I prayed that God would waken my ear to listen to this dying soul. When Millie did speak, I learned to pose questions that invited further conversation: "Can you tell me more about this?" or "How does that make you feel?" I never interrupted her or talked about myself. As I sat by her bedside, I felt I was on holy ground.

After regular weekly visits and much listening to Millie, one day she looked at me and asked, "Why me? Why has God allowed this to happen?" I simply reflected her questions and replied, "It seems to me that you feel God has been unfair to let this happen." She nodded and responded, "It's so unfair for my life to be cut short and to have to leave Jim and my work." More silence. Softly, I said, "I know; that's hard to understand."

As Millie's condition worsened, silence punctuated my visits more and more. But I assured her I would be there for her and offered comforting prayers as I left. Finally, as the end drew near, Millie had to go to the hospital. Jim never gave up his hope that she would get well. I was present when she neared the end. Millie's slow breathing in and out provided the only sound in the room. I went home to rest briefly and returned to discover that Millie had died. With unashamed tears in my eyes, I stood with Jim in the silence. The only words he could muster were these: "This is life."

I learned so much from Millie's raw courage and honest faith. I learned how to keep a silent vigil with a dying person. As Meister Eckhart wrote, "There is nothing so much like God as silence. Silence provides time for our souls to be present." Silence also is simply being present to a dying person when words seem futile.

CONVERSATION STARTER
Is there anything you'd like to talk about? I am here for you, whenever you want and however I can be.

REFLECTIVE EXERCISE
Have you ever been with a loved one or a friend who is dying? How comfortable did you feel being with her or him? What lessons did that experience teach you?

When you prepare to visit someone who is dying, pray this prayer.

Compassionate God, be with _____ as she (or he) makes the journey from this life to the next. Surround her (or him) with your love. When the time comes, send your angels to take her (or him) to your heavenly home. Amen.

2 SMALL DEATHS PREPARE US

But Ruth said, "Do not press me to leave you. . . . Where you go, I will go; where you lodge, I will lodge; your people shall be my people, and your God my God. Where you die, I will die—there will I be buried.

—Ruth 1:16-17

Sue seemed puzzled. She served as the primary caregiver for her aged mother who was slowly dying at home. Her mother, Margaret, was greatly depressed and, despite the care given by visiting nurses, refused to accept the fact of her impending death. Sue accepted her mother's denial of death but felt the time had come to talk about death with her mother.

One rainy afternoon, Sue said to her mother, "Mom, can you recall some significant moments in your life when something ended, only to bring new beginnings?" Margaret's face brightened. "Oh, yes," she replied. "I'll never forget how hard it was for me to move from the country to a big city." At first I was angry at your daddy for making me leave our beautiful home and all our friends. I hated to say good-bye to familiar surroundings but soon learned to love the city with its big libraries and concerts, and I made new friends."

Margaret paused, as if deep in thought, and then went on to say, "You'll never know how hard it was for me, Sue, when your father left us and later married another woman. He left me to raise you children with little money and no job. I thought I would die. But after going to a Beyond Divorce support group, I learned to mourn the loss of my marriage and moved on. Now I realize God worked in a wondrous way. I met Harry at church. His wife had died. We married, and he became a wonderful stepfather to you children. But it's been so hard since he died." Sue sat in silence, for she too loved her stepfather and mourned his loss. She held her mother's hand as mother and daughter sat in mutual grief.

Then Sue said, "Mother, do you see that all those losses became new beginnings?" Margaret thought for a moment, and then replied, "Yes, all those losses were like small deaths, and I learned to move on to a new life. "

Sue asserted, "It seems to me that dying is what we do while we are living. The many small deaths prepare us for the big one."

Margaret had been a devoted Bible reader all her life. She reminded Sue of the story of Ruth who had left her home in Moab and gone with her mother-in-law to a strange land. She asked Sue to read the story of Ruth to her. When Sue finished reading the story, Margaret slowly whispered, "You know, Sue, that's my story. Ruth lost everything and began a new life. Is that what death is?" The silence that ensued was like a prayer.

CONVERSATION STARTER

Can you remember moments in your life when you had to face changes or transitions? Can you share one of those with me?

REFLECTIVE EXERCISE

We may not share the intimate history that generated the conversation between Sue and Margaret, but we can encourage positive reflection on life experiences. We can raise questions such as these:

- What were the happiest moments in your life? What turning points can you recall?
- What has been important to you?
- How would you like to be remembered?

The caregiver could record the answers and place them in a life storybook that the dying person can leave with the family as a legacy.

✑

Lord, help _____ **to recall moments of transition in her (his) life and to learn from them how to deal with present challenges. Amen.**

3 NO USE DENYING IT

From that time on, Jesus began to show his disciples that he must go to Jerusalem and undergo great suffering at the hands of the elders and chief priests and scribes, and be killed, and on the third day be raised.

—MATTHEW 16:21

Many family members believe it best to conceal the knowledge of a loved one's impending death. They worry that talking about death with the loved one will create fear and cause the person to give up and want to die. Often I hear family members say, "You will live and get well, so don't give up"—even if the dying person knows that death is imminent.

Tom found this conspiracy of silence to be true in his situation. His family refused to talk with him about his death. If he tried to broach the subject, his children would say, "Oh, Daddy, don't talk like that. You're going to be fine." When the doctor suggested hospice care for Tom, his children refused, saying hospice was like a kiss of death. Tom acquiesced to his family's wishes, even though he knew death was near. He even told the nurse, "Don't say anything to my family about dying. They won't face it, and I don't think they can handle it."

In reality, Tom had come to accept his death, while his family members were stuck in denial. His family's denial of death mirrors a society and culture that often view death as something shameful and horrible. Death remains the "elephant in the room," a topic so volatile that people avoid it and push it from their consciousness. They laugh at the words of comedian Woody Allen, "It's not that I am afraid to die, I just don't want to be there when it happens."[1]

After his experience at Caesarea Philippi, Jesus began to speak openly about his death. Peter would have none of this death talk and blurted out, "God forbid it, Lord! This must never happen to you"

(Matt. 16:22). We appreciate Peter's concern for Jesus, but we don't tell people facing death not to think about it. The disciples' shock at Jesus' announcement of his death made them unable to hear the words "and will rise again." Tom, like Jesus, had to walk the solitary road of facing death because he had no family members who would talk about it with him.

Encouraging signs indicate that some people do want to discuss death. One new phenomenon is the emergence of Death Cafes, where people meet to talk about the taboo subject. They believe that the more they talk about dying, the more they add to life. But denial of death remains rampant.

CONVERSATION STARTER
This may be hard for you, but will you tell me about your illness and how serious you feel it is?

REFLECTIVE EXERCISE
Knowing the right moment to acknowledge the reality of approaching death is not easy. In the best of circumstances, family and friends may have discussed their mortality in earlier times and feel better prepared to speak openly when one of them reaches the threshold of death. That's rarely the case, though. We often must courageously bring the subject out in the open.

- How could Tom have gained family support for his belief that he was indeed dying?
- What role could the doctor have played in helping the family accept Tom's condition?

Dear God, grant me grace to put aside my own will and listen with an open heart to what my loved one is trying to tell me. Amen.

4   LIVING ON THE EDGE

Come now, you who say, "Today or tomorrow we will go to such and such a town and spend a year there, doing business and making money." Yet you do not even know what tomorrow will bring. What is your life? For you are a mist that appears for a little while and then vanishes.

—JAMES 4:13-14

Bill was a community icon, twice named "Man of the Year" in his town. He was the driving force to build a new library. When he joined my retirement community, he continued working for the welfare of the town.

Bill and I sat together in the chapel preparing to lead a devotional over the closed-circuit TV. Bill, who was eighty-eight years old, said to me, "Dick, we all live on the edge here. We never know when our time will come." Then he turned to speak into the microphone and began reading the story of the prodigal son from Luke 15. He never finished it. He read these words about the prodigal's return, "He was dead and is alive again," and then said, "Oh, no." The Bible dropped to the ground as Bill's head slumped. He had suffered a major aneurysm, from which he never recovered. He died three days later. His sudden death startled us all, especially his wife, Ann. As she stood before his coffin, Ann said, " The nerve of him to leave me like this. I never had a chance to say good-bye." Ann died a year later, having never recovered from her grief.

Sudden deaths create circumstances that leave traumatized survivors. Ten percent of us will die suddenly and unexpectedly. Unlike slower deaths that allow a time for good-byes, sudden deaths permit no time for closure. Nor are they restricted to older people like Bill. It happens to people at any age.

Bobby, a teenager who had decided on ministerial vocation, was returning home from a high-school basketball game. He swerved to avoid an oncoming car and hit a tree. The impact threw Bobby from the car, and he died instantly. At his funeral, his mother threw herself on his coffin and cried, "O God, my God, why did you let this happen?" At that time, I was a young pastor in a church, but the words of that grief-stricken mother have haunted me ever since.

Bonnie, a former coworker in a nursing home, wrote to convey her unhappy news. On a rainy night, a truck careened out of control, struck the car containing her daughter and granddaughter, killing both. I sent a note expressing my condolences. Bonnie's reply read as follows: "I will never get over this. I loved them so much. They were the joy of my life. Now I am hard as stone."

The book of James reminds us of life's brevity. We live on the edge and are like a "mist that appears for a little while and then vanishes." Death in the life cycle does not always come as a bright autumnal end, as "a shock of grain . . . in its season" (Job 5:26). We may rage, compromise, and even welcome death; but if it comes prematurely, it is always an unwelcome visitor. Realizing that we live on the edge and that death may come at any moment encourages us to make each day count. Knowledge that life is not forever and has its limits teaches us to use our time wisely and lovingly.

CONVERSATION STARTER (*for a family member*)

I know _____'s death is a real shock. Are you able to talk about it?

REFLECTIVE EXERCISE

Have you ever experienced the sudden death of a loved one or friend?

- How did that make you feel?
- How does the memory of that death linger even now?

Almighty God, you have given me the swift and solemn trust of this life. Teach me to make each day count by doing justice, loving kindness and walking humbly with you. Amen.

5 WANTING TO DIE

Why should light be given to the weary, and life to those in misery? They long for death, and it won't come. They search for death more eagerly than for hidden treasure. It is a blessed relief when they die, when they find the grave.

—JOB 3:20-22, NLT

I first met Robert in the community dining room. He sat by himself, and as my wife and I walked by, I noticed he seemed forlorn. He had just moved into the community and needed a friend, so I sat down beside him. We discovered that both of us had come from North Carolina, and we had much in common. As he choked back the tears, he said, "My wife promised to come with me, so we could be near our daughter and her family. But my wife died, so I had to come alone. It's so hard to be alone in a strange place without her. People don't know how it feels unless they experience it." I sat quietly, letting him express his grief, and told him we would stay in touch.

Later, as Robert's health declined, he moved from assisted living to personal care. I often visited him. He sat in a room cluttered with family photos and old magazines. On one occasion he told me, "I have no desire to live. Life is nothing without Mary."

I responded, "You really miss her and wish she was still with you."

"Yes," he replied. "My arthritis pain is getting worse every day. I serve no purpose in life. I think some people live too long."

Even visits from his daughter and family did not cheer him up. At some point when I visited Robert he did not want to talk and stayed in his bed. He stopped eating and simply waited for death. I realized he was shutting down. I sat with Robert in his final days. He had given up. In a short time, he died.

We live in an age that is extending life. In this past century we have added years to our lives at an unprecedented rate. So we take the suggested steps to extend our lives—diet, exercise, stress reduction.

A long life can be a blessing if persons are in reasonably good mental and physical health—and if they have a reason for living.

But what happens if longer life brings relentless frailty in mind and body? Then it becomes a curse as we suffer from unrelieved pain, and every day becomes a challenge to survive. When people believe they have outlived their usefulness—and no longer have a reason for being or a sense of being needed—is longer life a blessing or a curse?

In Robert's case it was a curse. In the words of Job (3:21-22), he longed for death, which came as a blessed relief. A good life entails more than simply living longer. When I visit nursing homes, residents often pose the question "Why has the Lord left me here so long?" "Why is it so hard to die?" "Why can't I just go to sleep and not wake up?"

My only response: "I don't know." As I exited the facility, I recalled a question a doctor once raised: "Why is it that you religious people want to prolong life when there is no quality of life and you believe there is a better life beyond this one?" Good question.

I felt no sadness when I attended Robert's funeral. His wish to die was granted. He lived a long life in this good world, and now he was reunited with his wife and at home.

CONVERSATION STARTER
I know it must be hard to battle this illness. What makes you feel hopeful? In what areas are you experiencing despair?

REFLECTIVE EXERCISE
- How would you have approached Robert's situation?
- What could you say to comfort the daughter who wanted her father to live longer?
- How have you known long life to be a blessing or a curse?

Loving God, help me to know when the time is right to help my loved one fight to stay alive or to help a loved one face death. Amen.

6 WHEN IS THE RIGHT TIME TO DIE?

For everything there is a season, and a time for every matter under heaven: a time to be born, and a time to die. . . .

—ECCLESIASTES 3:1-2

As a hospice chaplain, I spent a lot of time with Chuck, a patient in an in-house hospice facility in North Carolina. Chuck had battled prostate cancer that had metastasized to his bones for some time and finally agreed with his family to call in hospice. One day he looked at me with searching eyes and asked, "How much time do I have left?" His doctor had not told him the answer, but an untrained nursing assistant had told him he had two weeks to live. What was Chuck to believe? The author of the book of Hebrews wrote, "It is appointed for mortals to die once" (Heb. 9:27), but the time of our death is not for us to know. I confess I submitted my personal information to an online questionnaire that would tell me the time of my death. My answer read as follows: "Sorry, you have expired. Have a good day." Two things we can say about death with certainty: We will die, and we cannot say when or how we will die.

Clock time (*chronos*) differs from "right time" (*kairos*). In our culture we live by clock time, a sequence measured by hours and dates and events in proper order. The imminence of death teaches us the value of qualitative time (*kairos*) where we live in the moment, forgetting measured time. Chuck wanted to know the time (*chronos*) of his death. No one knows. But we can give a dying person meaningful moments (*kairos*) in the time that remains.

When we spend quality time with a loved one who is dying, we don't realize that time has passed. The fifth-century Rule of Saint Benedict includes this instruction: "Day by day remind yourself that you are going to die."[2]

So each day we cherish time as sacred time. Whether these days be as long as the shoreline or few and fleeting as the morning dew matters little. What matters is not when we die, but how we choose to live in whatever time we have.

In many ways death is like time. As Saint Augustine wrote, "What, then, is time? If no one asks me, I know what it is. If I wish to explain it to him who asks me, I do not know."[3] My brother, John Crossley Morgan, wrote these words:

> TAKE TIME
> Take time, any time, to consider this:
> Any time you will have no time
> And will be nothing in time.
> Or be in some other time.
> One moment you are here, another gone.
> If you take this seriously, make some time your time.
> Make every day a celebration.[4]

CONVERSATION STARTER

How do the words of the poem, "One moment you are here, another gone" make you feel?

REFLECTIVE EXERCISE

Give some thought to your own life, and ask yourself which is more important: how long you will live, or how you will give meaning to each day?

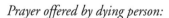

Prayer offered by dying person:

God who hears my every prayer, help my unbelief. If you want me to keep fighting, give me courage. If my fight is done, give me peace. Amen.

7 BEFORE NIGHT COMES

All of us must quickly carry out the tasks assigned us by the one who sent me, for there is little time left before the night falls and all work comes to an end.

—John 9:4

Jan, a quiet person who lived in my community, and I shared a passion for history and the traits of introversion. Even after her retirement, she continued her dedicated work at Children's Hospital in Pittsburgh. When a housekeeper found her dead in her apartment, that news sent shock waves through our community. We learned that Jan had leukemia but had not told her family. Only her closest friend knew, and Jan had sworn her to secrecy.

Often people want to fulfill some wish before their deaths. Jan wanted to be present for an award from Children's Hospital for her many years of service. Three days after receiving that award, she never woke from sleep. I had the privilege of leading her memorial service. At that service I quoted these lines from a hymn:

> Come, labor on! No time for rest,
> till glows the western sky.
> Till the long shadows o'er our pathway lie,
> And a glad sound comes with the setting sun,
> "Well done, well done!"[5]

For Jan, the shadows of death had come, but she could be assured that the Lord of life would say of her life and service, "Well done, well done."

Jan's death served as a strong reminder to us all that life is short, and we need to be prepared to face death at any time. That is the meaning of Jesus' words in the Gospel of John. Just as people must do their work while it is day and before darkness falls, so his ministry had to be in the "day" before the darkness of evil descended upon him and nailed him to a cross.

I hope it doesn't seem too morbid to acknowledge that death is an ever-present reality. Even as we face death's reality, we do not cease to love life. In fact, it helps us prioritize what is important in our lives. But we need to know and understand that we will not be here forever, that someday each of us will "check out."

Donald W. Shriver, former President of Union Theological Seminary in New York, in his book *On Second Thought* writes, "Once a grandchild of three reminded us at a dinner table, 'You are going to die, and so am I, too.'" Shriver adds, "How she became aware of death, I do not know. It was a precocious awareness from which parents want to protect their young."[6] The poignant awareness of a little child and the sudden death of a friend remind us that we too will die.

CONVERSATION STARTER (*for family*)

Is it hard for you accept _____'s death, especially when you knew nothing about it?

REFLECTIVE EXERCISE

If your doctor told you that you had an incurable disease and your time was limited, would you choose to shield your family and friends by not telling them the truth? If not, whom would you tell?

If you knew that you were to die soon, what would you say to those who love you? Say it now.

Eternal Friend, give me grace to live each day as if it were my last. Help me realize that death is always near, especially when I lose a dear friend. Give me grace to accept whenever death comes. Amen.

MAKING PREPARATIONS

After Jesus had spoken these words, he looked up to heaven and said, "Father, the hour has come. . . . "

—JOHN 17:1

8 BEING PREPARED

Then the kingdom of heaven will be like this: Ten bridesmaids took their lamps and went to meet the bridegroom. Five of them were foolish and five were wise. . . .the wise took flasks of oil with their lamps . . . and those who were ready went with him into the wedding banquet. . . . Keep awake therefore, for you know neither the day nor the hour.

—MATTHEW 25:1-2, 10, 13

Everyone desires a peaceful death. Most persons' ideal for the end of life involves settled affairs and a good and fulfilling life with few regrets. Four of five persons say they would prefer to die at home, although in reality, most die in nursing homes or hospitals. In the United States only 20% of us die at home. Until the middle of the twentieth century, most Americans died at home rather than in medical or long-term institutions. Today, medicine has forced people to decide where and how they die. If they choose to live as long as possible, regardless of quality of life, medical technology will extend life and prolong death. Some may die in nursing homes with palliative care; others may die at home with hospice workers. What matters is that the dying receive safe and gentle care during this time of need.

However, when persons do not make their wishes known through advanced directives, family battles around deathbeds are all too common. Mildred, an eighty-five-year-old woman in my church, had never given thought to her death plans. She became seriously ill and could not speak for herself. Her admssion to the hospital created a division in her large family. Some wanted to keep her alive as long as possible and demanded that she remain on the ventilator and maintain the feeding tube. I knew some of the family dynamics, and several of the ones who wanted "heroic measures" for their mother were estranged from her. I wondered if they wanted to keep her alive out of guilt. Other family members who had maintained a close relationship with their mother felt the time had come to pull the plug and let her die in peace.

One afternoon as I approached Mildred's room, I heard loud, dissident voices. I entered the room and told the children, "I think it is disrespectful to argue in your mother's presence" and suggested they continue their heated conversations elsewhere. A short time later Mildred was taken off life support, and she died within a few hours.

We need to make plans for our dying while we can—writing them out and giving them to our families and the attending physician. Jesus' parable of the ten bridesmaids speaks to this need. Five of the bridesmaids had prepared for the coming of the bridegroom. They had removed the burnt wicks and added oil to their lamps and provided light to escort the bridegroom to the bride's house. The maidens who had not prepared were left outside in the darkness The parable does not blame the five foolish maidens. The contrast focuses on those found ready when the call comes and those who are not. The parable intends to encourage our readiness for the Lord's second coming; it can also apply to the hour of death. Its message: Be prepared!

CONVERSATION STARTER (*for family*)

As your [pastor, family member, hospice chaplain] may I suggest we have a family conference to talk about _____'s wishes?

REFLECTIVE EXERCISE

Does the uncertainty of a family member's final wishes make you more willing to form your own?

Lord, life's demands catch us so off guard that we fail to make plans for the end of life. Grant us clear minds to make these plans and offer compassion and understanding to family members to assure they're carried out. Amen.

9 FINAL CHOICES

Then Joseph said to his brothers, "I am about to die. . . . So Joseph made the Israelites swear, saying, "When God comes to you, you shall carry up my bones from here."

—GENESIS 50:24-25

Martin Luther said, "Every man must do two things alone; he must do his own believing and his own dying." Death is a complex mystery and each person's death is unique. I have given a lot of thought to my dying wishes and have recorded my choices in a document called "Five Wishes."[1] This action on my part relieves my family of making these choices for me when that day arrives. Yet only one in five Americans has completed advanced directives or written a living will.

The patriarch Joseph made his wishes about his death arrangements known to his family. By his act Joseph reaffirmed his faith in the God of Israel. Joseph knew he would not be among the Israelites in the flesh when they left Egypt and marched to Canaan. But his bones would accompany them. He felt certain that the end of redemptive history is not a "coffin in Egypt" but fulfillment of God's promise of deliverance from bondage. Moses took the bones of Joseph when the Israelites began the journey to Canaan (Exod. 13:19). When they entered the Promised Land, they buried Joseph's bones in Shechem (Josh. 24:32). Hebrews 11, the roll call of faith, singles out Joseph's command as his most significant act of faith. It was "by faith [that] Joseph, at the end of his life, made mention of the exodus of the Israelites and gave instructions about his burial" (Heb. 11:22).

Joseph exemplifies the willingness to plan his death as a witness to his faith. The document "Five Wishes" allows people to do the same by recording the following information: (1) The person who will make decisions for you when you can't. (2) The kind of medical treatment you do or don't want, including decisions about life support. (3) How comfortable you want to be. (4) How you want people to treat you, which could include dying at home; if possible, bedside prayers, pictures, etc. (5) What you want your loved ones to know, including burial plans and your ethical will. Your ethical will makes note of what you want your family to remember about your wisdom and values. Signing "Five Wishes" automatically revokes all previous durable power of attorney grants and any and all previous wills you may have made.

Among my wishes are these: To have the courage to die without "heroic measures" to keep me alive beyond quality time. To die at home with palliative care from hospice, so I can die without pain and in relative comfort. To die on my bed in the room where I now live, with mementos of my spiritual journey and photos of my family around me. To listen to classical music and readings from scripture.

I have recorded my requests in the document "Five Wishes." Filling out "Five Wishes" has given me a sense of peace; it helps my family members know my wishes when the time comes for my final journey. It is a valuable aid to making final plans.

CONVERSATION STARTER
Who would you wish to see or be informed about your situation? What thoughts have you given to recording your wishes now?

REFLECTIVE EXERCISE
Put yourself in the place of your loved one who is dying. Have you made your wishes about end-of-life care known? If not, would you consider using the "Five Wishes" document? If so, information is available in the Notes.

Father, give me wisdom to decide what is best for the end of my life and the courage to tell my family. Amen.

10 WHAT ABOUT HOSPICE?

[The Samaritan] went to him and bandaged his wounds, having poured oil and wine on them. Then he put him on his own animal, brought him to an inn, and took care of him.

—LUKE 10:34

I often visited the home of Frank, a close friend, and his wife, Mary, who was dying from leukemia. Frank engaged the services of a full-time nursing aide for Mary. The aide became Mary's constant companion. As time passed, Mary's situation worsened, and her physician recommended hospice care to Frank. Without talking with Mary, Frank, who liked to control everything, refused to consider hospice care. When I tried to tell Frank about the loving care hospice offered, he emphatically replied, "No way. Hospice means giving up. I just can't use the H word with my wife. If I did, she would give up and admit defeat." When I suggested that hospice would be a great help to him also, he replied, "I'm fine and don't want to discuss it anymore." End of conversation.

David, another friend and parish member, willingly called in hospice for his dying mother, Nancy. He agreed with her physician that hospice was the answer. At first, Nancy had loving care from hospice in her home. The hospice nurse empowered Nancy to make decisions that would ensure quality medical care and offered expert pain control. I visited Nancy often, read the scriptures with her, and offered prayers. Before I left her bedside, I quoted the words of Moses, "The eternal God is your refuge, and his everlasting arms are under you" (Deut. 33:27, NLT).

Nancy told her family that hospice helped her to live more fully in her final days. Later, as her situation become more acute, Dave moved Nancy to an inpatient hospice in the community. The hospice nurses maintained their constant care, and hospice volunteers came to sit with Nancy to give her family respite when they needed a break.

Nancy was comfortable, free from pain, and lived out her last days surrounded by loving care from hospice nurses and family. She died quietly as soft music played in the room. I was there and thought to myself, *This is the way to die.*

Dame Cicely Saunders, who founded St. Christopher's Hospice in Sydenham (about forty minutes from London) in the 1960s, expressed the heart and soul of this compassionate care for the dying in these words, "You matter because you are. You matter to the last moment of your life, and we will do all we can not only to help you to die peacefully, but also to live until you die."[2]

Hospice represents a positive response to modern medicine's depersonalization of a dying person. My long years of experience as a pastor and a chaplain ministering to dying persons has convinced me that hospice is an answer to prayer for those who are dying and for their families and caregivers. I have experienced hospice as a spiritual journey. Hospice can offer a wholeness that makes a powerful impact on the lives of caregivers, patients, and families alike.

CONVERSATION STARTER
Would you be willing for our doctor to talk about the availability of hospice care?

REFLECTIVE EXERCISE
What words and understandings would you use to encourage a loved one to pursue hospice care when suggested by a physician? Would you want hospice care?

Compassionate Christ, help me to show _____ that hospice can offer blessing in the final days; put the right words in my mouth. Amen.

11   COMPASSIONATE COMPANIONS

*Word came to Joseph that his father was ill. So Joseph went
to visit him, and he took with him his two sons, Manasseh
and Ephraim. When Jacob heard that Joseph had arrived, he
gathered his strength and sat up in bed to greet him.*

—GENESIS 48:1-2, NLT

I would like to have been present for that moment of joy,
remembrance, and blessing. Old Jacob, who thought his favorite son,
Joseph, had died, is himself dying in Egypt. When Joseph hears his
father is ill, he makes a visit to his beside and takes Jacob's grandsons
with him.

Ask people what they most fear about dying, and the universal
response tends to be dying in pain or dying alone. If the sting of
death is sin, the sting of dying is being alone. Mother Teresa affirmed,
"No one should die alone. . . . Each human should die with the sight
of a loving human face."[3] In some situations persons have outlived
their family and friends; they have no one with them as they die. Or,
it may be that for some reason, the only available family member
cannot be there. Sandra Clark, a registered nurse at Sacred Heart
Medical Center in Eugene, Oregon, recently initiated No One Dies
Alone (NODA), a ministry to connect volunteer caregivers with
dying persons who have no family to be with them as they make their
final transition.[4] Volunteers offer compassionate companionship to
the dying so that they are not alone in their last hours.

I have discovered that the dying often begin to draw the circle
in around themselves as death approaches. These circles become less
and less expansive, until only close family and hospice volunteers
or nurses are there. My inner circle as I die would consist of my
immediate family, a few friends, and the hospice nurse and/or
chaplain.

Recently, a member of our retirement community left the hospital to die in his own apartment. The family put him on a bed in the living room as if on display. People sauntered in and out of the room. Some lingered but many spent time with idle talk. I felt very uncomfortable with that setting and have made it clear that I want only a few compassionate companions present. I want the privacy of being alone with God and my chosen few as I leave this earth.

Contrast this scene with another. Tim is dying in dignity in his own apartment. His children and their spouses are in the chapel singing some of his favorite hymns on the closed-circuit TV that is piped to his room. As the end neared, his family left the chapel and stood around his bed singing hymns of praise with joy as he departed. Tim's death bore powerful witness to the Resurrection and to his faith.

CONVERSATION STARTER
You told me your greatest fear is dying alone. Can you say more about that?

REFLECTIVE EXERCISE
Dying persons deserve the option to choose whom they want present as they die.

Whom would you choose? Why?

What (or whom) do you not want be present? Why?

Prayer offered by dying person.

Dearest Friend, I thank you for dear friends who stand with me and offer their care. I cherish your gift of friends. Help me to lean on them as I lean on you. Amen.

12 PLANNING YOUR FUNERAL

*Then Asa slept with his ancestors, dying in the forty-first year
of his reign. They buried him in the tomb that he had hewn
out for himself in the city of David. They laid him on a bier
that had been filled with various kinds of spices prepared by the
perfumer's art; and they made a very great fire in his honor.*

—2 CHRONICLES 16:13-14

The writer of Ecclesiastes sounded somewhat morbid when he
wrote, "It is better to spend your time at funerals than festivals. For
you are going to die, and you should think about it while there is still
time" (Eccles. 7:2, NLT). Most people would much prefer going to a
party than to a funeral. At this stage of my life, I am attending many
funerals of retirement community neighbors. At each service, I think
about my own death and funeral plans.

Since I prefer a simple funeral service, I cannot relate to King Asa's
elaborate funeral plans; but I commend him for making them. We
need to give careful thought to what happens to our bodies after our
death and to the kind of funeral or memorial service we want. Our
attention to these details relieves our families of the responsibility.

Furthermore, the process of working out the order of service and
the music dispels anxiety. We can then file these wishes with our wills
and give copies to our families and the funeral director of our choice.
We can also decide whether our bodies will be buried or cremated.

The baby boomers, the largest generation in American history,
now face the last third of life. They have spent their lives changing
cultural ideas and practices and will assuredly be change agents for
end-of-life practices. They will create a "natural death" movement.
Death will become de-medicalized and once again be viewed as a
natural event that can take place at home. Most will prefer cremation
and save expensive funeral costs.

Some time ago I made my funeral plans, which are available for my family and my funeral director.[5] There will be no "viewing" of my body in a funeral home. My body will be cremated, and the ashes put in an urn and taken to the cemetery. Since I occupied some space in this life, so will there be a place for my cremains. It will also provide a quiet spot on earth where family can visit and remember my life. After a brief service, the minister will offer the words "earth to earth, ashes to ashes, dust to dust," followed by a prayer of committal.

If cremation is the preferred mode of burial, decisions will have to be made about interment of the ashes. If we delay making funeral plans, family members will make them for us; some persons prefer that approach. Most people prefer to make their own plans.

CONVERSATION STARTER

Do you want to talk about funeral plans, or do you want your family to make those decisions?

REFLECTIVE EXERCISE

Has your loved one who is dying made funeral plans? If not, is it possible to ask about them? Have you made your own funeral plans? If not, will you consider pursuing such a matter?

Lord, as I make my funeral plans, may they reflect the values and beliefs of my life. Amen.

13   CONCERN FOR FAMILY

When Jesus saw his mother and the disciple whom he loved standing beside her, he said to his mother, "Woman, here is your son." Then he said to the disciple, "Here is your mother." And from that hour the disciple took her into his own home.

—JOHN 19:26-27

Jesus' last recorded words while dying on the cross were for others. Jesus died as he lived. He forgave sinners and comforted the hurting, forgiving the penitent thief as well as those who brought about his death. Jesus expressed concern for Mary, his mother. He died as he had lived, more concerned for others than himself. He told John to take care of his mother after he was gone. Joseph, Mary's husband, was already dead, and Jesus, as the eldest son, had been supporting Mary and the family. As a widow, Mary required the care of a male relative, so Jesus assigned that care to his disciple John. Jesus, in the throes of agony on the cross, showed compassion for a mother whose son was dying. At the cross a new family was built—not based on blood ties but on common faith.

No one could begin to emulate Jesus' selfless love. However, concern for the family also surfaces in these situations. "How will they manage when I am gone?" is a question many dying persons ask. Debilitating depression keeps some who are dying from talking to their loved ones about the future. The dying may see no future in this life. When people asked me, "What do people who are sick and dying talk about with the chaplain?" I always gave the same answer. Mostly they talk about their families—parents, sons and daughters, brothers and sisters, because relationships are what matter.

We bring to our dying the person we have been in life. If a person lives well and shows concern for others, he or she will display that same concern while dying. My brother Howard shared some of the conversations he had with his wife, Judith, as she was dying.

I learned much about the essence of life while I helped her finish her life. . . . Most beautiful of all, the two of us had time in the evenings to remember special life events together. These were moments of unbounded joy. She was able to counsel me how to go on and live a happy life even without her. One day, near the end of her life, we agreed that there was both everything and nothing more to be said except that we loved each other so much and had been fortunate to have found each other. . . . I have been given a great gift, to be with a loved one who is dying; all the facades of the unneeded are dropped; the real life source surfaces as cleanly as a pure mountain stream. Death becomes a true friend, an enabler, to help one move on where pain and suffering are no more, and a new eternal dawn of indescribably perfect dimensions has arrived.[6]

Circumstances may prevent such an intimate conversation. Perhaps the dying person has no family, or depression precludes talking. At such time the church, the body of Christ, steps up to play a major role. The church is the faith community in which individuals who are dying can receive the comforting presence of caring church members. Or, if the person has no church home, then friends or volunteers may stand in the gap.

CONVERSATION STARTER
Is there anything else we need to say to each other? Can you feel assured we will take care of each other?

REFLECTIVE EXERCISE
Visualize final weeks with a loved one who is dying. What might be on their minds and hearts? What would you say to assure them of your ongoing care for them and yourself?

Prayer prayed with a dying one.
Father, who has set the solitary in families, we thank you for our families, especially when we suffer and face death. Help _____ to know that we will be OK and will be surrounded by family members and your constant care. Amen.

14 WHEN NO CONVERSATION IS POSSIBLE

I have been dismissed as one who is dead, like a strong man with no strength left. They have abandoned me to death, and I am as good as dead. I am forgotten.

—PSALM 88:4-5, NLT

Ruth's husband, Bill, had a massive stoke but survived. The weeks passed, and Bill slipped into vascular dementia as a result of the stroke. Ruth cared for him at home, but she experienced a sense of isolation since Bill seldom spoke. She told her friend, "I feel a deep sadness; it's as if Bill has died." Bill, for the most part, no longer recognized Ruth and didn't know any of his family. He would gain a few moments of lucidity when he seemed to recognize his wife, but he quickly disappeared into the fog that enveloped him. Ruth told her pastor, "It seems I am constantly in mourning because the Bill I knew is gone. It's like looking at a photograph of your husband that gets fainter and fainter until it becomes a blank page." Ruth seemed to be stuck in a limbo that had no immediate resolution. Ruth's grieving began before Bill's death as she watched him die in slow motion.

When Bill regressed to an infancy state and required constant nursing care, Ruth placed him in a nursing home. She continued to visit Bill, although he never recognized her. When Bill died, Ruth told a friend, "It's strange, but I don't feel any sadness now. My grief didn't begin the day Bill died. It began the day he was diagnosed with dementia. I lost my husband piece by piece; watching him gradually die with no conversation was far more horrible that viewing his dead body. In fact," she added, "Bill's death came as a great relief because I knew then he was a whole person once more."

As the incidence of Alzheimer's disease and other forms of dementia continue to grow, more and more people will face the issue of caring for persons with dementia who have lost their identity but not their souls. The author of Psalm 88 describes a person who is cut off from life, "dismissed as one who is dead." It is extremely hard to live with a person with whom you cannot converse.

However, the precious moments of startling clarity can flash like lightning. One man told me that his wife who had dementia and rarely spoke awakened him in the middle of the night. She hugged him and said, "I love you. Thanks for taking care of me." She then returned to her largely nonverbal state. These moments are rare.

Persons whose loved ones never suffer from dementia have the time to remember happy moments and relive life events. There is also time to say good-byes as the loved one makes her or his final journey. This option is usually nonexistent with persons who suffer from dementia except for those rare moments of lucidity. No reliving experiences or saying good-byes—only patiently being with the person, holding hands, and sitting in silence through the long days and nights until death comes as a gentle relief.

CONVERSATION STARTER

Holding the loved one's hand and looking into his or her eyes say, "I want you to know I am with you and will stay with you."

REFLECTIVE EXERCISE

Have you ever cared for a loved one with dementia? What was that experience like? Did ever you pray for his or her death?

Do you know a person who is caring for someone with dementia? If so, what support can you give them?

Lover of lost souls, you reached out with compassion to those who suffered the loss of their identity and often found themselves forgotten. Help them and us know that you never forget anyone. Amen.

15 STRENGTH FROM GETHSEMANE

[Jesus and his disciples] went to a place called Gethsemane; and he said his disciples, "Sit here while I pray." . . . And he said to them, "I am deeply grieved, even to death."

Then an angel from heaven appeared to him and gave him strength.

—MARK 14:32, 34 and LUKE 22:43

As the child of a Presbyterian minister, I still remember Heinrich Hoffman's portrait of Jesus in Gethsemane that hung on a wall in our living room. It left an indelible memory of Jesus agonizing in the garden. I next saw that portrait years later in the living room of my younger sister Mary. She was battling lung cancer, and the chemo treatments had taken their toll. I sensed that death was not far away, but she never gave up or lost her loving spirit. As I sat in her dying presence, I glanced at the portrait of Jesus in Gethsemane, which she had brought from our former home. As I directed our gaze to that remarkable portrait, we had an unplanned Bible study right then and there. Softly I said, "That picture tells us that Jesus struggled with his own dying and told his disciples that he was grieved unto death. Jesus showed that it was human to wish it would not happen."

I went on to tell my sister, "I just hate that this has happened to you, Mary." She smiled and replied, "Since I was diagnosed with cancer and faced all these treatments, I gain strength from that scene. I am blessed by having neighbors, a special friend, and hospice nurses to see me through this, and I know the Lord is with me. I'll be fine."

Our conversation continued as I commented, "I'm glad you can talk openly about dying and share your fears and concerns."

"Remember," she said, "I was the only one of the children present when Mother died. I had to call you in the middle of the night when Dad had his fatal heart attack. I've worked for many years as a psychiatric nurse and been with dying people, so death is no stranger."

I sat in awe of her courage and faith, having both qualities in more measure than I could ever possess if confronted with such a death sentence. She reminded me of a sentence that the Gospel writer Luke added to the account of Gethsemane: "An angel from heaven appeared to him and gave him strength." It made her realize that God gives special grace to the dying. In that moment the words of Paul came to mind, " I am convinced that neither death nor life, . . . nor anything else in all creation, will be able to separate us from the love of God in Christ Jesus our Lord (Rom. 8:38, 39).

Several months later, I called to check in with my sister's hospice nurse. She told me the end was near. My wife and I drove five hundred miles to be there before Mary died. She seemed barely conscious, but I believe she knew we were there. In a matter of minutes she smiled and went home to God. I stepped outside for a breath of air and to dry my tears. Darkness was descending, and streaks of light from the rising moon illumined Mary's front yard. I knew she was alive and well. She had kept the faith in her garden of Gethsemane and now had walked into the garden of Resurrection.

CONVERSATION STARTER
I know you are fully aware of your situation. Can we talk about it?

REFLECTIVE EXERCISE
Visualize a meaningful object (crucifix, rosary, old Bible) you would want to have with you as you are dying.

Pray this prayer with your loved one.
We know, Lord Jesus, that you are with _____
as she or he faces suffering and death. Direct our thoughts to your suffering on the cross. May that strengthen us to bear our pain. Amen.

FINDING CLOSURE

As for me. . . . the time of my departure has come. I have fought the good fight, I have finished the race, I have kept the faith.

—2 TIMOTHY 4:6-7

16 FOUR THINGS TO SAY

Let your speech always be gracious, seasoned with salt, so that you may know how you ought to answer everyone.

—COLOSSIANS 4:6

As death draws closer, conversations between family members and the loved one who is dying can become difficult. Loved ones want to help but may lack the training or forethought to know what to say. Or, they may worry about saying something that will make matters worse. However, when such conversations are approached in a loving way, the worst outcome would be realizing that such conversations are simply not possible. Yet, a common complaint from a dying person is, "My dying is lonely, and I need to talk; but everyone avoids the subject or changes the conversation." Family members and caregivers can begin the conversation, then wait for a response. As they do, they may be pleasantly surprised by the result. Family members can initiate conversation by knocking on the door of the person's heart. She or he must open the door.

We can do very little for the dying. We can make them comfortable. We can be with them through creative listening. At times silence may form the heart of conversation. But sometimes we need to speak words.

Dr. Ira Byock believed that four simple statements open the door for meaningful conversation between dying persons and their families or caregivers. He had taught hundreds of patients who were facing life's end to say four things:

Please forgive me.
I forgive you.
Thank you.
I love you.[1]

These four short sentences carry the core wisdom of what people who are dying have taught me about what most matters in life.[2] Our relationships both in life and death are what matter. In my being with dying persons and their families, these eleven words summarize what we need to say at any time but especially in our dying.

Thomas Carlyle, Scottish essayist and historian, married his secretary, Jane Welsh. His devotion to his work precluded his noticing his wife's ill health. Finally Jane was confined to her bed, but Carlyle had little time to stay with her or to attend to her. After several years Jane died. Carlyle went upstairs to Jane's room and sat in the chair next to her bed, the chair for which he had had so little time. Friends found Carlyle back at the churchyard kneeling in the earth at the side of Jane's grave. He cried, "If only I had known. If only I had known."

CONVERSATION STARTER

I am here to be with you and listen. Do have any thoughts you want to express?

REFLECTIVE EXERCISE

Give the dying person ample time to respond to Byock's four statements, then share some of your thoughts about them. What other statements could serve the same purpose?

Dear God, be present with my loved one and with me as we try to talk about what really matters in our lives. May we realize that when we feel helpless and unworthy, your Spirit helps us in our weakness and prays for us. Amen.

17   I FORGIVE YOU; PLEASE FORGIVE ME

You must make allowance for each other's faults and forgive the person who offends you. Remember, the Lord forgave you, so you must forgive others.

—COLOSSIANS 3:13, NLT

Even in the closest families, people can harbor resentment, grudges, and other negative feelings toward one another. People who are dying often feel a need to make things right with significant others. Some people tend to think that asking forgiveness means you were the only one who did something wrong. However, your loved one may have wronged you too. One of the most important tasks for a dying person is to wipe the slate clean and say to family members, "I forgive you." In *The Tibetan Book of Living and Dying,* Sogyal Rinpoche writes the following:

> All religions stress the power of forgiveness, and this power is never more necessary, nor more deeply felt than when someone is dying. Through forgiving and being forgiven, we purify ourselves of the darkness of what we have done, and prepare ourselves more completely for the journey through death.[3]

Craig had been estranged from his sons. After their mother died, they were unhappy when he remarried. They kept a polite distance from their father and rarely visited him. When they learned their father was in hospice and had a short time to live, the dividing walls broke down. They visited regularly and shared memories. Distance gave way to closeness, estrangement to reconciliation. Like the father of the prodigal son, Craig embraced his sons with forgiving love. He even asked them to forgive him for not initiating a closer relationship. Forgiving one another freed them from the emotional baggage they had carried for some time.

In David Lynch's film *The Straight Story*, we learn the true story of Alvin Straight's 1994 journey across Iowa and Wisconsin on a tractor. When Alvin hears that his estranged brother, Lyle, has suffered a stroke, he decides to visit him and make amends before he dies. Alvin, obviously ill, builds a trailer, stocks it with food and other necessities, and hitches it to his tractor. Helped by others on the way, Alvin finishes the 240-mile journey. As both brothers face their own death, they reconcile and offer mutual forgiveness for longstanding hurts.

Forgiveness given and received does not always bring reconciliation nor does apologizing always bring about a positive outcome. But for the dying person and the family member who have carried this baggage for years, the experience of forgiveness can be a redemptive one. Long-term rifts are forgotten as the reality of death looms large. Old resentments and severed relationships are healed.

Finally, when people say, "Please forgive me," they can forgive themselves and let go of the guilt they have carried.

CONVERSATION STARTER

When have I hurt you? Please forgive me. Can you forgive yourself for mistakes you have made or things left undone?

REFLECTIVE EXERCISE

Take a moment to reflect on your life and recall when you hurt someone by word or deed. Then ask God for forgiveness and forgive yourself.

Consider praying the Lord's Prayer together. Pause briefly after saying, "Forgive us our trespasses as we forgive those who trespass against us." When finished, simply sit in silence for a few moments.

18   THANK YOU AND I LOVE YOU

I thank my God every time I remember you, constantly praying with joy in every one of my prayers for all of you. . . . Beloved, let us love one another, because love is from God; everyone who loves is born of God and knows God.

—Philippians 1:3 and 1 John 4:7

Five simple words expressed by and to a dying person can mean more than any others. Saying thank you can bring joy and peace to dying persons and their caregivers. Baptist preacher Joel Gregory writes that when members of the Masai tribe of West Africa express thanks, they sit on the ground in front of the person to whom they are indebted and then say, "I sit on the ground before you."[4] Sitting by the bedside of a dying person is an expression of gratitude for what that person means to you. Then a dying person can express his or her appreciation to caregivers saying two words, "Thank you." Meister Eckhart wrote, "If the only prayer you ever say in your whole life is, 'thank you,' that would suffice."

It is also the time to say I love you. Millard knew that Anne loved him, but she rarely told Millard that. Millard was diagnosed with leukemia; after several treatments his situation worsened. Anne was always there for him, keeping him at home—which was his wish—and daily caring for his needs.

Millard and Anne had many conversations at his bedside. On one occasion, he reminded Anne of the words of Tevye in *Fiddler on the Roof*, when he asked his wife, "Golde, do you love me?" Golde protested his question and proceeded to tell him all she did for him in their twenty-five-year marriage. Tevye persisted, "Golde, do you love me?" Finally she replied, "I suppose I do." Tevye responded, "I suppose I love you too." Anne got the message. She said the three magic words to Millard, and he told her how much he loved her.

Henry Drummond, a great scientist in the late nineteenth century, reflected on his life and wrote the following:

> I have seen almost all of the beautiful things God has made; I have enjoyed almost every pleasure He has planned for man; and yet as I look back I see standing out above all the life that has gone, four or five short experiences when the love of God reflected itself in some poor imitation, some small act of love of mine, and these seem to be things which alone of all one's life abide.[5]

Some people can say the words "I love you" to their loved ones. Others cannot. Yet when the end of a relationship seems imminent, no other words mean more. Saint John of the Cross said it well, "In the evening of life we will be judged on love alone." In those evening hours, when dark shadows fall across our world, three things remain: faith, hope and love—but the greatest of these is love.

CONVERSATION STARTER
Can you recall special people in your life for whom you are grateful? Are there people to whom you wish to say, "I love you"?

REFLECTIVE EXERCISE
If appropriate, encourage the family members to speak aloud expressions of love and gratitude to their dying loved one. This may foster a response from the dying one.

～

If a pastor or chaplain is present when these words of love are spoken, she or he may pray this prayer.

Loving God, we stand on holy ground at this precious moment when expressions of love are given. May the memory of this moment remain always in the heart of those who care, and be a foretaste of your heavenly kingdom when love is above all. Amen.

19 FIVE REGRETS OF DYING PEOPLE

I am still not all I should be, but I am focusing all my energies on this one thing: Forgetting the past and looking forward to what lies ahead . . . .

—Philippians 3:13, nlt

As life comes to an end, especially as people reflect on the past, they cannot help but have some regrets; no one is perfect. Who of us has not wished to do things differently, this time "getting it right." Bronnie Ware, a nurse who worked in palliative care, listened as dying patients expressed their regrets. The five most common regrets dying patients mentioned were these: (1) I wish I'd had the courage to live a life true to myself, not the life others expected of me. (2) I wish I hadn't worked so hard. (3) I wish I had had the courage to express my feelings. (4) I wish I had stayed in touch with my friends. (5) I wish I had let myself be happier.[6]

In a real sense, these regrets become words of wisdom from those who are dying. They remind those of us who still live that we can make choices that will allow us to end life with fewer regrets. We can address these issues while time remains. As we face the inevitability of death, we can shift our priorities. Bronnie Ware wrote, "The regrets they shared left me determined to not feel the same at the end of my own time, whenever that was."[7]

In writing to the church at Philippi, the apostle Paul expressed genuine regret for having been an enemy of the Christian faith who persecuted followers of the Way. I can imagine Paul's guilt over his participation in the murder of Christians and his attempts to destroy the church. Then Paul encountered the risen Christ and became a follower of the faith he once tried to extinguish. Later in life, he managed to move beyond those sad memories and to focus on being Christ's disciple in the present and future.

I resonate with these top regrets expressed by dying people. At midlife, counseling helped me cast off the "old self" of parental expectation to become the person I truly was. Before that midlife conversion, I was repressed and withdrew from people, afraid to express my feelings for fear of rejection. So I lived in my own shell. I regretted that I was not free to be who I was. Counseling helped me learn to state my feelings with no concern about rejection or disapproval from others. I knew that in my earlier life I had devoted myself too much to my work and neglected my sons. I lived to regret those lost years. However, in later life I developed a strong relationship with both sons and even became a mentor to my grandchildren. I still regret that I denied myself happiness by being too ambitious and driven to succeed in my chosen career. Only later did I take time for myself and my family and find real joy in a less-driven life.

However, if you are at the end of life, with little time to rewrite your story, consider making peace with your regrets and forgiving yourself. The God who forgave the apostle Paul for his crimes against the church will surely forgive you.

CONVERSATION STARTER
What regrets in your life would you like to talk about?

REFLECTIVE EXERCISE
To which of the top five regrets of the dying do you relate? What steps can you take to deal with those regrets?

Pray this prayer with your loved one.
Loving God, you search me and know me, and understand me better than I understand myself. Help me realize that your grace is sufficient to accept my regrets. Amen.

20 NO REGRETS

Strength and dignity are her clothing, and she laughs at the time to come.

—Proverbs 31:25

Esther taught me how to die. A faithful member of my congregation, Esther learned she had inoperable cancer and had a few weeks to live. Hospice came to offer palliative care. Esther was ready to die and had already given away possessions to make her final journey easier. She talked openly about her dying and said good-byes to her husband and family. On one occasion she laughed as she said to me, "I guess I surprised everyone by not dying today."

I had planned to go to Buffalo to perform my son's wedding but felt I needed to be available for her last days. Esther told me, "You need to go. If I die while you're away, I'll be fine. I have trusted God all my life, so I can surely trust him when I die." I made the trip, and Esther did not die before I returned. I believe she waited so I could be there when she left this world. "Strength and dignity are her clothing, and she laughs at the time to come."

Grace was an old country woman who was always full of laughter and witty sayings. I loved her dearly. After she fell and injured her neck, Grace had to wear a cumbersome "halo," but that burden didn't defeat her or break her spirit. Every time I visited her, her contagious faith and delightful spirit inspired me. I never knew what she would say or do next. One night a woman across the hall from Grace's room kept screaming, "Help me. Help me." When Grace could stand the screaming no more, she yelled, "Be quiet! We all need help here." The first time I met Grace, I asked her name. She replied, "Same as it's always been." I knew then we would become friends.

Grace's life was coming to its end, but I wasn't there when she died. The next day I walked into her room and saw the vacant bed. I watched aides stuff her belongings into bags. They could clean out her room, take her name off the door, but the inner light in her life would never be extinguished.

In one of my last visits, I sat by her bedside, held her hand, and listened. I can still hear the last words she ever spoke to me, "The good Lord knows best, but I'll be ready when he calls. I just hope I go to sleep and never wake up. I won't be here long, but I'll see you in heaven." That halo she wore became a symbol of her angelic ministry to everyone who knew her. "Strength and dignity are her clothing, and she laughs at the time to come."

Esther and Grace both died with no regrets. They had lived full and rich lives. I learned from them how to die unafraid and with healing laughter. It seemed as if they had turned the page on one chapter in the book of their lives and were ready to begin the next one. I hope I can have a small measure of their faith when my time comes, so I too can "laugh at the time to come."

CONVERSATION STARTER
What memories do you have of people who faced death with courage? Tell me about them.

REFLECTIVE EXERCISE
Have you been with people like Esther and Grace, who died with strength and dignity? Relive those moments.

Prayed with families after the death of a loved one.

Gentle Mother God, we thank you for sending loved ones into our lives who bless us not only while they are alive, but even when they die. We pause now to hallow their memories and to give thanks for them. Amen.

21   LIFE-REVIEW CONVERSATION

Remember the days of old, consider the years long past.

—DEUTERONOMY 32:7

As terminal illness brings people closer to death, they may begin a life review: a time of reflection on the meaning of their lives. Recording loved ones' life biographies gives their story to the family and helps the dying persons recognize the meaning of their lives and affirm that their lives have made a difference. Many persons who recount near-death experiences tell that after seeing the warm light and walking through a tunnel, they see their lives flash before them in a moment.

For many years I recorded life stories and led workshops so others could learn the skills of life-review conversation. I remember recording the life story of Abby, a retired nurse, whose days ended in a nursing home. Abby was piecing a quilt while I recorded her life story in several sessions. When we finished our time together, Abby stated, "My life is like one big patchwork made up of pieces. Each story is a piece of the quilt block. When I pieced together my story, it became a beautiful quilt, and sharing my story helped me see the pattern of my life. Now I can die in peace."

Sam was dying and wanted me to listen to his life story and record it for his family. When we began, Sam noted, "You get to the point in life when it's important to look back: for me, there is no future." When we finished our life-review conversations, Sam said, "As I look at my life, it's better than I thought. I've lived my life and done the best I could. It's better than I thought."

Mercy lingered in a nursing home as her life dwindled to a few days. I learned about her childhood in Holland, living under Nazi occupation. I believed her special story needed to be recorded. Mercy told about the difficulties of surviving the harsh treatment of her oppressors. I gladly preserved her story of courage and faith and gave the written record to her family.

CONVERSATION STARTER

If you could leave one message to a handful of people who are most important to you, who would they be and what would you say?[8]

REFLECTIVE EXERCISE

Along with your loved one, look at the following list of questions, as well as the closing suggestion. Select a few questions and set aside thirty minutes to an hour for life-review conversation. Although you could use a tape recorder or voice recorder, it may be easier to write your loved one's answers down and later transcribe your notes. You can then make a notebook or scrapbook for your loved one and her or his family.

- Looking back at your life, what were some of your greatest satisfactions?
- What were some of the major turning points in your life? What difference did they make?
- Name some people who have been spiritual friends for you across the years. How did they help you?
- What health issues did you face and how did you cope with them?
- What gifts can you claim that will live on through you?
- If you could live your life over again, what would you change?
- How would you like to be remembered?
- Summarize your life in five sentences.

Almighty God, you are the beginning and the end. You created me and have been with me all my life. I pray that you will help _____ to remember his or her life story and share it with me, confident "that the one who began a good work among you will bring it to completion by the day of Jesus Christ." (Phil. 1:6). Amen.

22 LEARNING TO SAY GOOD-BYE

When [Paul] had finished speaking, he knelt down with them all and prayed. There was much weeping among them all; they embraced Paul and kissed him, grieving . . . that they would not see him again.

—Acts 20:36-38

Saying good-bye is often difficult. No one wants to say good-bye to a loved one. Recall a time when a son or daughter or other loved one left home, and you said good-bye with a lump in your throat. Or recall a moment when you said good-bye to people you loved when you moved to another town. Somehow we know that an ongoing relationship will be tenuous.

We read this touching moment when Paul said good-bye to the elders of the church at Ephesus. They knew they would not see one another again. What a heartfelt farewell! They knelt for prayer and wept. Then they embraced Paul and escorted him to the ship, perhaps watching as he disappeared from sight.

Good-byes between dying persons and their loved ones are especially difficult because they are terribly final. Some people face the hardship of trying to reach closure after a sudden or unexpected death when time has run out to say good-bye. Sometimes dying persons linger in depression and can't face their approaching death or discuss it with family. However, some persons who face their death find the courage to say their good-byes. As a hospice volunteer, I often witness people's delaying their death in order to achieve some goal, such as holding a new grandchild or attending a wedding.

I recall one remarkable moment when a woman near death gathered her family around her beside. They remembered good times as a family, and their cherished memories dispelled the room's darkness. They then were able to say their good-byes—a touching moment of reality. After their good-byes, they asked me to pray.

Somehow God gave me the words, "God of mercy, even before a word is on our tongues, you know it altogether. We thank you for the courage and faith of this family as they said their good-byes. Help them know that all good-byes can become new hellos when they see each other in a different setting where there are no good-byes."

My friend Ronald Vaughan expressed it well when he wrote these lines:

> I told you once that at my dying bed
> Your face would be the last thing I would know.
> But now I think that what I should have said,
> Is take my hand and I can safely go.[9]

CONVERSATION STARTER

We have often said good-bye to each other. Are you able to say good-bye now?

REFLECTIVE EXERCISE

Let your mind wander back to moments when you had to say good-bye, whether it was sending a son or daughter off to college, leaving friends when you relocated, or sitting at the bedside of a dying parent. How did that make you feel?

God, help us remember that our saying good-bye not only expresses love but conveys the meaning of the word itself, "God be with you." Amen.

23 LETTING GO

Jesus said to her, "Mary!" She turned and said to him in Hebrew, "Rabbouni!" (which means Teacher). Jesus said to her, "Do not hold on to me."

—JOHN 20:16-17

We practice the art of letting go while we live. At times we have to let go of a relationship or work of significance. Every night we practice letting go when we release ourselves to sleep and to the mysterious place of dreams. As we age, we let go of youth, health, and sexual attractiveness. Death is the final letting go of all that we are, the final selflessness. And it constitutes the final letting go by family who offer their loved ones permission to let go and die.

That permission giving is difficult for many people. Sometimes those who are dying don't want to leave their loved ones behind. But our attachment to those who are dying can cause unnecessary heartache and make it harder for them to let go and die peacefully. There comes a time when we must say to loved ones, "I won't cling to you any longer. I set you free to go home to God."

The Easter morning encounter between Mary Magdalene and Jesus is a classic story of letting go of the past so the future may come. In her joy at seeing Jesus she reached out to touch him. Mary tried to hold on to the Jesus of Nazareth, whom she remembered and loved. But Jesus said, "Do not hold on to me," Mary would have to learn that the Jesus whom she could touch in his earthly life would only be known as a presence in her heart. So too, loved ones whom we know in this life will depart, but they can become a living presence in our hearts.

I have often believed that a good analogy of letting go in the dying process is much like a trapeze artist. The flyer climbs the steps of the ladder and takes hold of the bar suspended between two ropes. This bar is a trapeze. Across the way is another person, the catcher, who hangs from another trapeze with his knees. His hands are free, reaching out and ready to catch the flyer. As the two artists swing back and forth, there comes a moment when the flyer lets go, suspended in midair. The flyer can do nothing to help himself or herself. It all depends on the catcher. Just as the flyer loses momentum, the catcher comes near and grabs the flyer with a sure and steady grip. All is well. So it is when we die; we let go of all we are, even life itself. In the empty space of an unknown world, steady, nail-scarred hands reach out to grab us. We are the flyers, and God is the catcher. So our lives end with the prayer Jesus prayed as he breathed his last and went home to God: "Father, into your hands I commit my spirit."

CONVERSATION STARTER
Can you let go now and be open to what lies ahead?

REFLECTIVE EXERCISE
How does the image of flyer and catcher make you feel about dying? Does it help to soften the fear of dying?

Incorporate the words of D. H. Lawrence into a prayer for the loved one who is dying:

Be careful, then, and be gentle about death.
For it is hard to die, it is difficult to go through
The door, even when it opens.

Dying Moments

Now we see in a mirror, dimly, but then we will see face to face. Now I know only in part; then I will know fully, even as I have been fully known.

—1 Corinthians 13:12

24 UNSEEN TO US, REAL TO THEM

Therefore, since we are surrounded by so great a cloud of witnesses. . . .

—Hebrews 12:1

Dying persons often seem to be in two worlds at once: in the present moment and somewhere else. They may talk or gesture to people who aren't visible to others in the room. My sister, Mary, in her last hours told us that she saw family members who "came" to her. Hospice nurses, Maggie Callanan and Patricia Kelley, in their book *Final Gifts* note the following, "What we term Nearing Death Awareness is a special knowledge about—and sometimes a control over—the process of dying."[1] These authors mention the way hospice patients develop a glassy-eyed look that appears to look through us. They use symbolic images such as travel, saying words like "Where's the map," "It's time to get in line," or "When does the train leave?" in their attempts to convey that the time has come for them to journey from this life.

In my final telephone conversation with my brother-in-law, Drue offered a classic example of a symbolic image. He had cared tirelessly for my sister in her final days on earth. He told me, "I accomplished my last mission: caring for Pat. Life is empty without her. I am ready to 'belly up.'" At first I didn't understand what he meant but later realized he was actually saying, "It's time to die." A week later Drue died; my niece told me his last words were these: "Death is part of life. No one lives forever."

Mary Anne Sanders, in her book *Nearing Death Awareness*, suggests a powerful image of a dying person straddling the fence between this life and the next. "Nearing Death Awareness behavior is the fence, with this physical life on one side and an unknown, new dimension on the other. The dying, in straddling the fence, can look back at their lives in retrospect and preparation, yet see glimpses over the fence of the numinous places they are about to travel to."[2]

These mystic, near-death experiences vividly exemplify what the author of Hebrews calls "the cloud of witnesses." People of faith surround the Christian community of any age. Do we then find it hard to believe that this "cloud of witnesses" hovers at the bedside of a dying person as she or he stands on the brink of crossing over to the other side? Ron Wooten-Green, in his book *When the Dying Speak*, writes these words:

> As the dying process kicks into gear, the dying person often begins to see these shadows ever so clearly. As the dying process begins to accelerate, these shadows then become more and more real: real people (usually deceased) and real places. In the final stage, the shadows have become people and places, that are visible only to the dying person who is approaching the end of life.[3]

Elisabeth Kübler-Ross, Swiss-American psychiatrist, has written, "In general, the people who are waiting for us on the other side are those who loved us the most. You will always meet those persons first."[4] Her words offer consolation and hope for the dying.

CONVERSATION STARTER

When have you experienced the closeness of loved ones who have died? Tell me about them.

REFLECTIVE EXERCISE

Which family members who have died would you like to "see" in your last hours? What religious or spiritual person would you want to see in your last hours?

❧

Gracious God, may _____ feel the surge of pure joy when the veil is lifted and she (he) glimpses again the living faces of departed family and friends. Amen.

25   WHEN THE VEIL IS REMOVED

For now we see in a mirror, dimly, but then we will see face to face. . . . But when one turns to the Lord, the veil is removed.

—1 Corinthians 13:12 and 3:16

I have known only a few moments in my life when I experienced an epiphany, a breakthrough; when I perceived reality from a new and deeper perspective. One such moment occurred in Wales, outside the ruins of the ancient Tintern Abbey monastery.

I rose before dawn and sat on a hillside near the river Wye, where I could see the ruins of the monastery, the home of monks now long gone. As the sun rose, it cast a brilliant light, and the early morning mist dissolved to a golden glow.

For a brief moment the veil separating the living and the departed became very thin, and I felt transported into another time and place. I could hear the monks chattering as they went about their daily tasks. I could hear them chanting their prayers at the altar. Time dissolved into a past now present. I was no longer sitting on a hillside by the river Wye but experiencing the life of the monastery. The poet William Wordsworth also had a sense of another world as he too sat on a hill outside Tintern Abbey: "I have felt a presence that disturbs me with the joy of elevated thoughts, a sense sublime." (From "Lines Composed a Few Miles above Tintern Abbey, on Revisiting the Banks of the Wye during a Tour, July 13, 1798").

Maggie Callanan and Linda Kelly are hospice nurses who pioneered the idea of Near Death Awareness from their caring for over a thousand dying patients. They believe that the dying often glimpse another world. "Rather than being in this world one moment, gone from it in the next, then jerked back to life, the dying person remains in the body, but at the same time becomes aware of a dimension that lies beyond."[5]

The martyr Stephen, of whom it was said, "They saw that his face was like the face of an angel" (Acts 6:15) experienced these two existences as he was dying. "He gazed into heaven and saw the glory of God and Jesus standing right hand of God. 'Look,' he said, 'I see the heavens opened and the Son of Man standing at the right hand of God!'" (Acts 7:55-56). Is it, then, hard to believe that when persons die in faith, God will grant them an awareness of another world and a peace that passes all understanding?

There is no better prayer than this: that our loved ones have such awareness and peace when they die.

CONVERSATION STARTER

What can you tell me about any dreams or visions you have had in recent days or nights?

REFLECTIVE EXERCISE

Can you name places in your experience where God was very real and present? What would you say to a dying one who claims to see "beyond the veil"?

We thank you, God, for the mystery beyond this life, a reality we believe but cannot see. Help us to walk by faith, not by sight. Amen.

26 RING DOWN THE CURTAIN

Six days later, Jesus took with him Peter and James and his brother John and led them up a high mountain, by themselves. And he was transfigured before them, and his face shone like the sun, and his clothes became dazzling white. Suddenly there appeared to them Moses and Elijah, talking with him.

—MATTHEW 17:1-3

Peter, James, and John were not dying, but they had the unusual experience of seeing Moses and Elijah returned from the dead. It was a moment of transfiguration for Jesus and of transformation for these three disciples whose lives would never be the same. No recorded account mentions any queries about the experience, but Jesus' words about rising from the dead puzzled them.

As a hospice chaplain, I visited Olivia, an eighty-eight-year-old woman suffering from Alzheimer's disease. Olivia lived in her own world. Although I visited her often, she never knew my name—or hers either. At times her speech was garbled and incoherent. Once I caught part of a sentence she spoke, "It's time to get my ticket for the show." I had no idea what she meant. I knew that before she developed Alzheimer's disease, she would share with me her love of opera. Her happiest memories revolved around attending operas in Charlotte, North Carolina.

When the hospice nurse told me that Olivia was near death, I had a flash of insight. I recalled that one of her favorite operas was Verdi's *La Traviata*. I recorded portions of the opera and played them for her as I sat quietly by her bedside. Olivia's face showed a trace of smile as she listened intently. When Pavarotti sang, "Let's drink from the joyful cup," her words sounded as clear as a bell: "Ring down the curtain. The opera is over." It seemed as if she already had been transported to another time and place. I then understood her earlier words, "It's time to get my ticket." In her own way she was telling me the time had come for her to die and move to the next stage of her life journey. I have long believed that people with dementia are evolving angels, indicating just how thin the veil is that separates the spirit world from ours. The disciples experienced life beyond the curtain in their mountaintop encounter. So Olivia, despite suffering from Alzheimer's disease, "saw" beyond the curtain.

At Olivia's memorial service, we played that same chorus from *La Traviata*, and somehow I knew Olivia was singing with the angels. Her joyful cup had overflowed.

The curtain of her life had fallen. But she had begun a new scene on the stage of a new world.

CONVERSATION STARTER

Can you remember special moments in your life when God was very near and real? If so, I would love to hear about them.

REFLECTION

Have you ever heard a dying loved one talk about taking a trip and use such images as "It's time to get in line" or "buying a ticket" or "where's the map?" How did you respond?

Gracious God, we thank you, for everything in this world brings awareness of your presence. Especially we praise you for music that nourishes our souls, that lingers in our mind and heart, and lifts us beyond this world to a world of peace and joy. Amen.

27   FINAL BREATH

Abraham breathed his last and died in a good old age . . . and was gathered to his people. His sons Isaac and Ishmael buried him in the cave of Machpelah.

—GENESIS 25:8-9

The family huddled around Paul's bed in the intensive care unit. He had lived a full life and had sung a solo in church at age ninety. Now this old man had wearied of the struggle to live and lay dying in the hospital. He gasped for breath as the family watched the monitor. The family had never discussed death with Paul. Paul didn't bring up the subject either. He didn't want to worry his wife and daughters. Earlier, as I visited Paul at home, he told me he wanted to die. He said, "I'm living too long. What's the point?" Yet, in this moment, Paul held on as his wife and daughters begged him not to die. I told his family, "Your father wants to die. He is tired and wants to go 'home,' but he needs your permission." Finally one of his daughters spoke up, "Daddy, it's OK to die. We'll be fine." With a smile on his face, Paul said, "It's beautiful over there"—and was gone.

What a strange scene we read about after Abraham breathed his last and died. His sons Isaac and Ishmael, once estranged by family dynamics, buried their differences as they lowered their father into the grave. We do not know if either of them had been present when their father died or if either of them said anything at his grave. Perhaps the scene played out in silence—two sons of the same father leaning on their shovels, with their father's dead body lying in the ground. All we know is that two brothers, fathers of nations, knew a chapter in their lives had ended. Another was beginning as they silently walked to their separate homes.

The loss of a parent leaves a void nothing can fill. Although it has been some time ago, I still feel the loss of my parents, as I became an adult orphan. I also experienced a heightened sense of my own mortality: Death was no longer a distant event but a present possibility.

My mother's death came as a blessing, ending months of painful struggle with Parkinson's disease and dementia. I had grieved her slow death long before she died. At my last visit with her I not only gave silent permission for her to die but prayed that God's angels would take her home.

My father's death was totally unexpected. He died from a massive coronary attack. Initially, I did not feel the same peace at his death as I did at my mother's. He was still active and, despite his age, lived a vibrant life. Later I realized he was spared inevitable suffering from heart disease and had fooled the medical system that would have held him hostage. Too often we hang on to our parents for our sake, not theirs. We allow them a graceful exit by telling them it is okay to die when that moment is near.

CONVERSATION STARTER
If you knew your parents were in their final moments, could you tell them, "It is okay to go" and say good-bye?

REFLECTION
If your parents are living, can you talk with them about death? If they have died, how has that affected you?

༄

Gracious God, for those of us whose parents are still living, help us to redeem the time with them. For those of us whose parents have died, give us grace to remember them with thanksgiving and joy. Amen.

28   OUT TO SEA

The time of my departure has come.

—2 TIMOTHY 4:6

Henry, at ninety-three years of age, was ready to die. Every time I visited him in the health-care center, I found him watching old Spencer Tracy movies. His daughter told me he watched them all the time. On one of my visits, Henry told me, "Dick, I am weary of life. I can't find any reason to live. Please pray that I die soon." He meant it. So, I knelt at his bedside and prayed, "Dear God, there is a time to live and a time to die. Your servant Henry has lived a good and full life and now wants to die. If that be your will, grant him his wish." Henry thanked me.

Several days later the nurse called to tell me that Henry had died. I hurried to his room, but the mortician had already taken his body. The TV was still on, and Spencer Tracy's film *The Old Man and the Sea* showed on the screen. Spencer Tracy played the role of the aging Cuban fisherman Santiago. Desperate to catch a big marlin, Santiago sailed too far out to sea. He caught the marlin, but sharks ate the big fish, even as Santiago attempted to turn them back. He arrived home with only the skeleton of the great fish. We cannot prevent death, but we can fight it as hard we can.

Henry had lost the will to fight death and had gone out to sea. Paul talks about his death in Second Timothy as a "departure": the rope is flung off, the anchor lifted, and the ship moves out of harbor to the wide and boundless sea, setting sail for worlds unknown. Paul envisions death as a moment for new adventure. The image seemed appropriate to Henry's "departure." The frailties and limitations of his advanced age had anchored him to a confined life in a nursing home. At death, the anchor lifted, and Henry sailed into unknown waters, crossing over Jordan, on his way home.

At Henry's memorial service the poem "Crossing the Bar" by Alfred Lord Tennyson was read. Tennyson wrote this poem in 1889, apparently thinking of his imminent death that came three years later in 1892. Henry had left this time and place and hoped to see his Pilot face to face.

Sunset and evening Star,
And one clear call for me!
And may there be no moaning of the bar,
When I put out to sea.

But such a tide as moving seems asleep,
Too full for sound and foam,
When that which drew from out the boundless deep
Turns again home.

Twilight and evening bell,
And after that the dark!
And may there be no sadness of farewell,
When I embark;

For tho' from out our bourne of Time and Place
The flood may bear me far,
I hope to see my Pilot face to face
When I have crossed the bar.

CONVERSATION STARTER

Are you weary of the struggle and tired of living? Can you talk with me about it?

REFLECTIVE EXERCISE

Consider reading selected verses of Tennyson's poem "Crossing the Bar" to one who is dying. If you do so, ask what assurance it brought to his or her situation.

Help us to believe, loving God, that dear ones who have passed from our sight are safe in your presence, forever at peace. Amen.

29 NOTHING TO FEAR

There is no fear in love, but perfect love casts out fear.

—1 JOHN 4:18

The dying man neared the end of his long and faithful life as a missionary to China. His son, Randy Taylor, told me that his father's last words were these: "There is nothing to fear." Those words have stayed with me for many years. If persons claim they don't fear death, they are fooling themselves.

I fear the actual process of dying more than what I believe occurs to the body after death. The possibility of dying from some terrible disease that causes endless pain or being bedridden and dependent on others because of my frailty evokes a fear of dying. When the moment comes, however, I do not fear what lies beyond. I await my future life with eager anticipation. "No eye has seen, no ear has heard, and no mind has imagined what God has prepared for those who love him" (1 Cor. 2:9, NLT). I willingly leave my end in the hands of a God who has lived with me through all my days, knowing that God's perfect love casts our fear.

My friend Wesley Stevens told a story about Ray, a United Methodist pastor in Houston, Texas, who had cancer. He lay in a hospital near death. Wesley visited his friend daily. Stevens wrote, "As time passed, Ray seemed to be gradually slipping off the bonds of the earth. On one visit, I think I must have prayed with greater intensity than usual. Later in the company of Evangeline and other members of the family, Ray said, 'Wesley bumped my car.' Then, in response to my questioning look, Evangeline explained that Ray had a model car hobby. His comment meant that he had already boarded the train bound for glory, when you came along and bumped his railroad car off the track. That evening Ray had a wonderful visit with his wife and family, and he died the next day."[6]

Henri J. M. Nouwen posed this question:

Is death something so terrible and absurd that we are better off not thinking or talking about it? . . . Or is it possible to befriend our death gradually and live open to it, trusting that we have nothing to fear? . . . Can we wait for our death as for a friend who wants to welcome us home?[7]

We can befriend death, believing that fear of death and judgment disappears when we know God's love. Although we may fear dying, belief in God's goodness and love gives us hope beyond our fears.

CONVERSATION STARTER
Can you share any fears you have about dying? Do you sense an assurance of life beyond death?

REFLECTIVE EXERCISE
Does the witness of these two pastors in their dying moments reassure you about death?

⬿

Lord, I do believe in a life yet to come full of joy, peace, and love. Help my unbelief and give me assurance when moments of doubt occur. Amen.

30   DYING: A GIFT FOR THE FUTURE

Then Jesus, crying with a loud voice, said, "Father, into your hands I commend my spirit." Having said this, he breathed his last.

—LUKE 23:46

Harold and I were good friends. We shared much in common. Both of us worked with older people. Harold had managed a personal care home before he retired, and aging had become the focus of my ministry. We shared physical problems, both escaping the possibility of cancer. Harold was a master builder, the mastermind behind the construction of a new building at our church. Harold also put his skills to work by helping erect a new senior center for the community.

When I retired and moved to another community, Harold and I kept in touch. His wife, Martha, called me one day and asked if I would come and pray with Harold. "He has taken to his bed," she said, "and thinks he will die soon." I hurried to their home, and we shared many stories from our church experiences. I prayed with Harold, and he seemed more content and at peace. I knew, however, his days were numbered.

One night at 3:00 a.m. I suddenly awoke and sat up in bed. I felt a slight brush on my face. Early the next morning, Martha called to tell me that Harold had died at that very hour. I know many explanations for that coincidence exist. But I believe Harold was saying good-bye as he entered "the city that has foundations, whose architect and builder is God" (Heb. 11:10).

I believe the dying leave a gift for the future. The meaning of their lives becomes clearer after they have died. As Jesus said, "Unless a grain of wheat falls into the earth and dies, it remains just a single grain; but if it dies, it bears much fruit" (John 12:24). When I think of Harold, what comes to mind is the gift of his life. Harold died, having lived a good and fruitful life with few regrets.

Harold epitomizes the words of the writer to the Hebrews about Abel, "He died, but through his faith he still speaks" (11:4). How much more did the death of Jesus become a gift for our future. He died as he lived, forgiving his enemies, offering grace to the penitent, and showing compassion for his family of faith. Jesus believed in the constant support of a loving God. His final words at death confirm his life of faith as he entrusted to God both his living and his dying: "Father, into your hands I commend my spirit."

CONVERSATION STARTER (*for family members*)
I know you must be proud of all that _____ accomplished. Want to talk about it?

REFLECTIVE EXERCISE
Look creatively at your life story. What will be your legacy? How will your family remember you?

———

I read John Donne's prayer (below) at Harold's memorial service, but it is a prayer that can be prayed with any dying person.

Bring us, O Lord God, at our last awakening into the house and gate of heaven to enter into that gate and dwell in that house, where there shall be no darkness nor dazzling, but one equal light; no noise nor silence, but one equal music; no fears nor hopes, but one equal possession; no ends nor beginnings, but one equal eternity; in the habitations of thy glory and dominion, world without end. Amen.

About the Author

RICHARD L. MORGAN, a retired Presbyterian (USA) pastor, stays busy writing and serves as a hospice volunteer in pastoral care at the Redstone Highlands retirement community near Pittsburgh, Pennsylvania. He and his wife, Alice Ann, reside in Redstone Highlands.

NOTES

Accepting Your Dying

1. Woody Allen, *Without Feathers* (New York: Ballantine, 1986), 106.
2. Timothy Fry and others, eds., *The Rule of St. Benedict in English* (New York: Vintage Books, 1998), 13.
3. Albert C. Outler, ed., *Augustine: Confessions and Enchiridion,* Library of Christian Classics, vol. 7 (Philadelphia: Westminster Press, 1955), 254.
4. John Crossley Morgan, *Thin Places* (Eugene, OR: Wipf and Stock, 2009), 42. Used by permission of Wipf and Stock Publishers. www.wipfandstock.com
5. Jane Laurie Bortwick, "Come, Labor On" (1859, 1863).
6. Donald W. Shriver Jr., *On Second Thought: Essays Out of My Life* (New York: Church Publishing Inc., 2010), 64–65. All rights reserved. Used by permission of Church Publishing Incorporated, New York, NY.

Making Preparations

1. The "Five Wishes" document can be ordered from Aging with Dignity, 305 Highlands Oaks Terrace, Tallahassee, Florida 32302-3841. (www.agingwithdignity.org), (850) 681-2010.
2. Quoted in Sandol Stoddard, *The Hospice Movement: A Better Way of Caring for the Dying* (New York: Vintage Books, 1992), 109.
3. Quoted in Paula A. Smith, "No One Dies Alone," *Pittsburgh Catholic,* 12/13/12.
4. Visit the website, http://peacehealth.com for further information.
5. See Richard L. Morgan, et. al. *Dear Brothers: Letters Facing Death* (Eugene, OR: Wipf and Stock, 2010), 50–60, for three examples of planned funerals.
6. Richard L. Morgan, *Meditations for the Grieving* (Eugene, OR: Wipf and Stock, 2005), 31. Used by permission of Wipf and Stock Publishers. www.wipfandstock.com.

Finding Closure

1. Ira Byock, *The Four Things That Matter Most: A Book about Living* (New York: Free Press, 2004), 3.
2. Ibid., 3.

3. Sogyal Rinpoche, *The Tibetan Book of Living and Dying: 20th Anniversary Edition* (New York: HarperCollins, 2002), 217.

4. Quoted in John Ortberg, *When the Game Is Over, It All Goes Back in the Box* (Grand Rapids, MI: Zondervan, 2007), 150.

5. Henry Drummond, *The Greatest Thing in the World and Other Addresses* (London/Glasgow: Collins, 1999), 54.

6. Bronnie Ware, *The Top Five Regrets of the Dying: A Life Transformed by the Dearly Departing* (Carlsbad, CA: Hay House, Inc., 2011).

7. Ibid., 226.

8. See Richard L. Morgan, *Remembering Your Story: Creating Your Own Spiritual Autobiography* (Nashville, TN: Upper Room, 2002), 162–68.

9. Thomas Ronald Vaughan, *Being Deaf at the Tower of Babel* (Swannanoa, NC: Ars Gratia Artis Press, 2013), 71.

DYING MOMENTS

1. Maggie Callanan and Patricia Kelley, *Final Gifts: Understanding the Special Awareness, Needs, and Communications of the Dying* (New York: Simon and Schuster, 1992), 21.

2. Mary Anne Sanders, *Nearing Death Awareness: A Guide to the Language, Visions, and Dreams of the Dying* (London: Jessica Kingsley Publishers, 2007), 121.

3. Ronald Wooten-Green, *When the Dying Speak: How to Listen to and Learn from Those Facing Death* (Chicago, IL: Loyola Press, 2001), 9–10.

4. Elisabeth Kübler-Ross, *On Life after Death* (Berkeley, CA: Celestial Arts, 2008), 9.

5. Callanan and Kelley, *Final Gifts*, 24.

6. Letter from Wesley Stevens to author, August 19, 2013. Used by permission.

7. Henri J. M. Nouwen, *Our Greatest Gift: A Meditation on Dying and Caring* (New York: HarperOne, 1994), xii–xiii.

SUGGESTED READING

Butler, Katy, K*nocking on Heaven's Door: The Path to a Better Way of Death.* New York: Scribner, 2013.

Byock, Ira. *The Four Things That Matter: A Book about Living.* New York: Free Press, 2004.

Callanan, Maggie and Patricia Kelley, *Final Gifts: Understanding the Special Awareness, Needs, and Communications of the Dying.* New York: Simon and Schuster, 1992.

Craddock, Fred, et. al. *Speaking of Dying: Recovering the Church's Voice in the Face of Death.* Grand Rapids, MI: Brazos Press, 2012.

Feldman David B., *The End of Life Handbook: A Compassionate Guide for Dying Loved Ones.* Oakland, CA: New Harbinger, 2007.

Kübler-Ross Elisabeth, *Death: The Final Stage of Growth.* New York: Simon and Schuster, 1969.

————. *On Death and Dying: What the Dying Have to Teach Doctors, Nurses, Clergy, and Their Own Families.* New York: Macmillan, 1968.

Morgan, Richard L., Howard C. and John C., *Dear Brothers: Letters Facing Death.* Eugene, OR: Wipf and Stock, 2010.

Nouwen, Henri J. M., *Our Greatest Gift: A Meditation for Dying and Caring.* New York: HarperOne, 1994.

Rinpoche, Sogyal, *The Tibetan Book of Living and Dying: 20th Anniversary Edition.* New York: HarperOne, 2002.

Sanders, Mary Anne. *Nearing Death Awareness: A Guide to the Language, Visions, and Dreams of the Dying.* Philadelphia, PA: Jessica Kingsley, 2007.

Scaglione, Paul A. and John M. Mulder, *The Spiritual Lives of Dying People: Testimonies of Hope and Courage.* Eugene, OR: Cascade Books, 2013.

Singh, Kathleen Dowling. *The Grace in Dying: A Message of Hope, Comfort, and Spiritual Transformation.* New York: HarperOne, 1998.

Swinton, John and Richard Payne, eds. *Living Well and Dying Faithfully: Christian Practices for End-of-Life Care.* Grand Rapids, MI: Wm. B. Eerdmans, 2008.

Ware, Bronnie. *The Top Five Regrets of the Dying: A Life Transformed by the Dearly Departing.* New York: Hay House, 2011.

Wooten-Green, Ronald. *When the Dying Speak: How to Listen to and Learn from Those Facing Death.* Chicago, IL: Loyola Press, 2001.

Wuellner, Flora Slosson, *Beyond Death: What Jesus Revealed about Eternal Life.* Nashville, TN: Upper Room Books, 2014.